COLLAPSE AND CHAOS

The Story of
the 2010 Earthquake in Haiti

BY JESSICA FREEBURG

CAPSTONE PRESS
a capstone imprint

Tangled History is published by Capstone Press,
1710 Roe Crest Drive, North Mankato, Minnesota 56003
www.mycapstone.com

Library of Congress Cataloging-in-Publication Data
Names: Freeburg, Jessica, author.
Title: Collapse and chaos : the story of the 2010 earthquake in Haiti / by
Jessica Freeburg.
Other titles: Story of the 2010 earthquake in Haiti
Description: North Mankato, Minnesota : Capstone Press, [2017] | Series:
Tangled history | Includes bibliographical references and index. |
Audience: Grades 4-6. | Audience: Ages 9-14.
Identifiers: LCCN 2016038586
ISBN 9781515736066 (library binding)
ISBN 9781515736103 (pbk.)
ISBN 9781515736349 (ebook (pdf)
Subjects: LCSH: Haiti Earthquake, Haiti, 2010—Personal narratives—Juvenile
literature. | Haiti Earthquake, Haiti, 2010—Biography—Juvenile literature.
Classification: LCC F1928.2 .F74 2017 | DDC 972.9407/3—dc23
LC record available at https://lccn.loc.gov/2016038586

Editorial Credits
Adrian Vigliano, editor; Kyle Grenz, designer; Tracy Cummins, media researcher;
Laura Manthe, production specialist

The author would like to thank Allison Insley-Madsen for sharing her story, her time,
and her understanding of the Haitian culture.

The publisher would like to thank LeGrace Benson for her help in the preparation of
this book.

Photo Credits
Alamy: Jan Sochor, 13, Zuma Press/David Snyder, 6; DVIDS: Photo by Chief Petty
Officer Joshua Kelsey, 52; flickr: joquerollo, 18; Getty Images: AFP/JUAN BARRETO,
27, AFP/LOGAN ABASSI, 34, AFP/ROBERTO SCHMIDT, 98, AFP/THOMAS COEX, 28,
AFP/Thony BELIZAIRE, 64, Jan Sochor/CON, 4, Owen Franken, 17, The Washington
Post/Carol Guzy, 97; iStockphoto: Claudiad, Cover; Polaris: Alex Quesada, 105;
Reuters: Eduardo Muno, 51, 66, Wolfgang Rattay, 85; Shutterstock: Jason Winter,
Cover Background; Wikimedia: U.S. DEPARTMENT OF DEFENSE/Fred W. Baker III, 103;
United States Navy/MC1 Joshua Lee Kelsey, 86

Printed in the United States of America.
10063S17

TABLE OF CONTENTS

FOREWORD

On January 12, 2010, residents of Haiti, located on the small island of Hispaniola in the Caribbean Sea, went about their usual routines. Living in one of the poorest countries in the world, with a history of slavery, brutal dictatorships, and deadly revolutions, many Haitians were working hard simply to earn enough to support their basic needs.

The markets in the capital city of Port-au-Prince were busy with men and women buying and selling goods. Voices speaking Haitian Creole, the French-based language used by most Haitians, floated through the markets like gentle waves. The streets were filled with greetings, casual conversations, and bartering. A steady flow of bodies and chatter filled the space as people carried on with business as usual.

Since only 50 percent of Haitian children went to school, many youngsters spent a typical day helping their parents or looking in nearby areas for work to bring home money. Those who attended school learned about their ancestors' proud accomplishments, including becoming the second nation in the Americas, after the United States, to secure its freedom from colonial rule. With a population composed almost entirely of descendants of African slaves, gaining independence made Haiti the first black republic in the modern world.

The Haitian people had weathered many natural disasters, including multiple hurricanes in 2008 that killed hundreds of local residents and demolished thousands of homes and businesses. But today, the sun shone brightly through a clear sky and there seemed no reason to worry as people continued with their work.

JUST ANOTHER DAY

1

A hillside community built on the hills above Port-au-Prince, 2009

Wismond Exantus

Port-au-Prince, Haiti,
January 12, 2010, 4:50 p.m.

Wismond reached across the counter and handed change to the women. The 24-year-old had been standing for several hours behind the counter at the small grocery store in the Napoli

Hotel in Port-au-Prince. He helped customers with their purchases as they passed through his line.

"Thank you," he said with a smile before wishing the customer a good day. *"Bon jounen."*

In Haiti, a good job was a precious thing. Wismond did not have to go far to find people in desperate situations brought on by poverty. The streets were full of people trying to sell anything that might bring them a little money — plastic water bottles refilled with juice, used baby clothes, and fruit. People walked among the traffic, wiping down vehicles as they passed, hoping the drivers might hand over a little money for the work.

He smiled at the next customer in line as she set her canned goods on the counter. *"Bonswa,"* he said, using the Haitian Creole word for "good evening."

The bell rang as Rosemary, her boyfriend, Romules, and her 21-year-old cousin, Stephanie, neared the André Malraux School.

They felt privileged to be students. They looked at attending classes as the doorway to a better life. For example, Stephanie's goal was to study medicine and become a doctor. Rosemary had no doubt her cousin could achieve this one day.

After Stephanie's aunt passed away, she moved in with Rosemary's family. Stephanie's quiet humor brightened the already joyful household, and the two cousins quickly became as close as sisters.

Rosemary and Romules paused at the gate, hoping they might settle their argument before Rosemary went into the school.

"Hurry, we still have a few minutes to study with the others," Stephanie called to them as she rushed toward the front door of the two-story schoolhouse.

"You'll make yourself late standing out here to bicker!" National college entrance exams were coming soon, and many students gathered in a classroom before regular classes to take advantage of every spare moment of study time.

"I'll be right in," Rosemary replied. "It should only take a minute to convince this stubborn boy why I am right and he is wrong."

"Or I'll pretend to agree quickly so you can get to class," Romules huffed.

Stephanie paused at the door and looked back at them both. "I'm not sure which of you is more stubborn," she said, smiling and shaking her head. Then she turned and hurried into the school.

Allison Insley-Madsen
Port-au-Prince, Haiti,
January 12, 2010, 4:50 p.m.

Allison sat on the exam table at her doctor's office. Her 6-year-old son, Jack, sat in a nearby chair playing a game. She hadn't planned to see the doctor this afternoon, but Dr. Maggie had insisted she come in to have a facial rash treated.

Accompanied by her bodyguard, Lamarre, Allison had changed course from a trip to the grocery store, and headed toward the doctor's office instead. Allison's family employed staff to protect them because of the high crime rates in and around the city. Despite her hopes for Haiti's future, she knew kidnappings and murders were far too common.

Allison had been in Haiti for several years. She came first in the spring of 1996, serving as a U.S. diplomat. Just one day after arriving in Haiti, she met her future husband. Although she left briefly to take a post in Paris, she returned, married, and settled in as a stay-at-home mother to their son, Jack.

"Your new building looks great," Allison said, glancing around the newly finished office on the second floor of the four-story structure.

"Thank you. My husband does nice work," Dr. Maggie replied. Her husband, a French architect, had designed the building. "Now you can lie back. We'll cover your eyes and start the treatment."

Allison settled back onto the table, shut her eyes, and allowed herself to relax.

Lexmark Aristide

Port-au-Prince, Haiti,
January 12, 2010, 4:50 p.m.

"When you are done with your homework, you can help me with dinner," Lexmark's father, Dieuveil Marceline, said. "I am going to feed your brother."

"OK," 12-year-old Lexmark replied as he looked up. His father stood in his bedroom doorway holding his baby brother.

Lexmark enjoyed most of his schoolwork and felt proud of himself for earning good grades. Education was very important to his family, and he knew he was lucky to be attending school. He knew many boys his age did not get to do so.

He heard the familiar creak of the rocking chair in the living room as his father settled into it to give the baby a bottle. Lexmark opened his textbook and turned to the chapter he had been assigned to read.

Laura sat on her bed, her back against her pillow and her bare feet stretched out in front of her. On her lap, she held a stack of research notes. She hadn't been sure what to expect when she arrived in Haiti from the United States to do research for her PhD six months earlier. She had seen news reports about problems in Haiti such as poverty, oppression, and injustice. These reports were in part what brought her to Port-au-Prince to study household workers and human rights.

Although hardships in Haiti were evident, Laura found the daily routines of those around her quietly predictable. Many of the men would go out each day, searching for odd jobs. She could count on seeing the young students washing their uniforms each night by hand. After dinner, families sat together to watch Mexican soap operas that had been dubbed over in French.

Laura had been touched to see the generosity of many Haitians who were happy to share what they could with her. The residents of this community, who in just a short amount of time had become her dear friends, shared their food and looked out for her as if she were a family member. She sat quietly reflecting on the notes she'd taken about her new friends.

The La Saline food market, Port-au-Prince

The steady buzz of people and traffic cut through the tropical air on a busy day at the La Saline food market. Evans was happy with the amount of rice and oil he had sold to customers as they made their way along the street.

He had just one batch of rice left to sell. His stomach was beginning to signal that it was almost dinnertime, and he looked forward to getting home and seeing his family.

A young woman approached him. "I would like to buy that rice from you, if I could," she said.

"Yes," Evans replied. "You will be my last customer today."

"Then you may go home until tomorrow," she smiled, counting out money for her purchase.

"*Mesi*," Evans said, using the Haitian creole word for "thank you."

"*Mesi*," she replied, turning and disappearing into the crowd of people passing by.

14

Dan Woolley sat beside his videographer, David Hames, in the backseat of the SUV as it bounced over the curving road, snaking toward the Hotel Montana. The two men had spent the day collecting footage of families participating in the Child Survival Program that would be used by Compassion International, the nonprofit organization Dan worked for. Their goal was to highlight the impact the program had on families in need.

Dan thought about how 85 percent of the population of Haiti lived below the poverty line. Half of the country's children under the age of 5 suffered from malnutrition. With those problems and the highest death rate of women giving birth in the world, there were many people in need of Compassion's programs.

One of the mothers they had interviewed that afternoon shared her dreams for her children.

She hoped they would finish school and that her son would grow up to be an architect. Dan hoped the Child Survival Program could make those dreams more of a reality for this mother's children. He was excited to be part of helping these families.

The SUV rolled to a stop in front of the hotel, and their guide, Ephraim, jumped out of the vehicle. As Dan and David stepped onto the curb, Ephraim grabbed each of them in a bear hug.

"We'll meet you back here tomorrow morning at 8:00," Dan said. He glanced at his watch. It was 4:52 p.m.

"We'll see you then," Ephraim replied. Then, climbing back into the vehicle, he waved as he started the engine and drove away.

Haitian merchants carry their wares
to sell at the market

FORTY SECONDS

2

The Hotel Montana sat in the hills above Port-au-Prince, providing guests a sweeping view of the city below.

Dan Woolley

Port-au-Prince, Haiti,
January 12, 2010, 4:53 p.m.

David and Dan walked through the lobby of the Hotel Montana and headed toward the open-air archway that led to the outdoor staircase.

With the fresh, tropical air and the bright sunshine, it seemed silly to miss out on the beautiful panoramic view of the city by riding in the elevator.

The peaceful beauty was interrupted by sudden, loud explosions that burst around them. The concrete rolled in waves beneath their feet, throwing them off balance.

"Earthquake!" David screamed.

Dan felt as if he'd been dropped into a battlefield, with bombs bursting in every direction. Within seconds of the first explosion, the walls around them began to crumble and fall. Dan looked for a desk to crawl under or a doorway to stand in, but there was nothing near him. The closest place he could find safety was the staircase they had been walking toward. He dove toward the bright blueness of the sky he could see through the archway as the archway swayed and crumbled before his eyes. And in an instant, the blue sky was replaced by smothering blackness.

Allison Insley-Madsen

Port-au-Prince, Haiti,
January 12, 2010, 4:53 p.m.

Dr. Maggie had left the room while the chemicals worked on Allison's face. The doctor's assistant stayed to monitor the progress of the procedure. Allison's eyes were still covered with the small goggles put on for protection when she felt a tremor shake her body. For a moment she thought her son was trying to get her attention by shaking the exam table. But when she removed the goggles and looked across the room to where her son had been sitting quietly playing his game, she saw him being tossed around helplessly. The floor beneath him rippled in great waves as if it were made of water. Allison was thrown from the table onto the floor.

Wismond Exantus

Port-au-Prince, Haiti,
January 12, 2010, 4:53 p.m.

When he felt the floor of the Napoli Hotel grocery store tremble violently beneath him, Wismond knew he needed to think fast and find a safe place. Knowing there was a desk just a few feet from where he stood, he turned and tried to hurry toward it. His body flopped around as the undulating floor battled against him. He fought to control his movements while the walls around him popped and buckled from the force of the moving earth.

"Dear God, save me!" he cried as the walls of the four-story hotel fell around him, leaving him trapped in utter darkness.

Rosemary Pierre

Port-au-Prince, Haiti,
January 12, 2010, 4:53 p.m.

Rosemary and Romules were still arguing outside the school when the ground began to rumble. The street rippled beneath her feet, causing her to fall to the ground. Romules' feet came out from under him, and he fell beside her.

Rosemary looked toward the school her cousin Stephanie had entered just moments earlier, but her view of the building was completely clouded by dust. The roar of concrete cracking and caving in on the buildings in every direction seemed to drown out the startled cries of frightened people being tossed about by the shifting road.

Lexmark Aristide

Port-au-Prince, Haiti,
January 12, 2010, 4:53 p.m.

As Lexmark turned the page in his textbook, he felt his bed shake violently. He dropped his book and looked toward his bedroom door.

"Papa!" he yelled, but his voice seemed to get lost in the sound of cracking concrete. The rippling waves that rolled across his bedroom floor tossed his small bed like a tiny boat in a huge ocean. He was thrown onto the ground and tried to scramble toward the door, but before he could reach it, the walls of his bedroom crumbled around him. Then the roof of his home crashed down above him. He knew instantly that he was trapped.

Laura Wagner

Port-au-Prince, Haiti,
January 12, 2010, 4:53 p.m.

When Laura felt the telltale vibrations of the earthquake, she managed to make it to the door between the hallway and the kitchen just off her bedroom. As the world shook around her, she realized what little control she had of her own body as she tried to brace herself in the frame. She didn't feel fear, just wonderment at the surprising course her quiet afternoon had taken.

And as the walls fell in around her, she thought how surprised she was to be dying like this.

René Préval

Port-au-Prince, Haiti,
January 12, 2010, 4:53 p.m.

The ground rippled beneath President René Garcia Préval's feet as he stood beside his wife, Elisabeth, in front of their private living quarters in the National Palace. They were just preparing to walk in when they felt the first tremors beneath their feet. Instinctively, they both jumped back from the building, hoping to avoid being hit by dangerous falling debris. Seconds later, as they stood there trying to keep themselves safe, they saw the beautiful white structure quiver and crack as parts of its walls gave way to the turbulent shaking.

The sound of the crumbling palace was echoing from all around President Préval as many of the structures on the streets nearby seemed to collapse simultaneously. Most of these buildings were surely filled with people, helplessly trapped in the massive chaos of the sudden destruction.

Within seconds, the second floor of the palace had pancaked into the first floor. President Préval's stomach dropped as he realized his country was being quickly ravaged by a force of nature. There was nothing he could do.

Evans Monsignac

Port-au-Prince, Haiti,
January 12, 2010, 4:53 p.m.

Evans watched the woman to whom he'd just sold his last batch of rice disappear into the crowd. Just as she was swallowed by the people moving down the street, the earth began to ripple and the sea of shoppers and vendors began to rise and fall with the concrete waves.

Evans had little time to take in what was happening before the roof of the ramshackle awning under which he had set up shop broke apart like a clay pot dropped on a hard floor. He fell to the ground. As dust swallowed the bright sunshine of the day, Evans felt the weight of a wall come down upon

In the aftermath of the earthquake, survivors did what they could to help those in need and gather what they needed to live.

him, pinning him to the ground. Flat on his back, Evans tried to move to the left and then the right, but he was hopelessly stuck. As buildings collapsed into the market a large chunk of concrete barreled toward him. Unable to move his lower body, he could do little more than cover his face with his hands.

"Oh, Lord," he cried out. "I'm dying!"

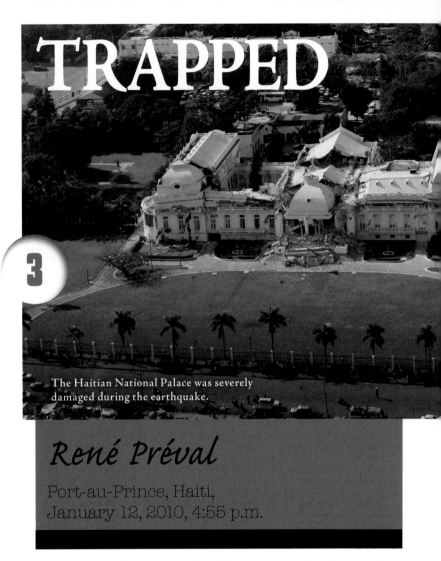

TRAPPED

3

The Haitian National Palace was severely damaged during the earthquake.

René Préval

Port-au-Prince, Haiti,
January 12, 2010, 4:55 p.m.

It was clear from the devastation that loomed in front of President Préval and Elisabeth that the earthquake had caused serious damage to the surrounding area. Préval knew he had to act, but

the shock of what had just happened seemed to hold him frozen in place.

"Are you all right?" Préval asked his wife as they picked themselves off the ground that had rippled mercilessly beneath them just moments before.

"I am," Elisabeth replied, still trembling with fear.

Préval looked around the streets near his home. It was clear from what he could see that the damage was vast.

"I must go," Préval said.

"Yes, go!" Elisabeth said.

Préval jogged toward the road behind them, where a motorcycle taxi driver was steadying himself as he remounted his vehicle. Préval waved at him, and the man quickly motioned for him to climb on.

Am I dead? The thought raced through Dan's mind as he blinked into the blackness. He was crouched, the crumbled mass of the hotel all around him. His leg throbbed, and as he tried to move it, he realized his foot was pinned beneath the debris.

Then the voices calling for help began to cry out from the rubble in every direction. He couldn't tell where they came from, whether they were above him or somewhere on the same level.

"David!" Dan called out. The last he had seen of his friend, David was standing to his left. He tried to look for him, but the darkness around him was so complete he could not even see his own hand in front of his face. With no sense of sight, it was impossible to make sense of where he was. For a moment, he wondered if he had been blinded somehow when the 145-room hotel crashed down on top of him.

"David!" he yelled again. He called out, over and over, the panic growing inside him each time. He sucked in deep, gasping breaths filled with dust. His lungs felt as if they were coated in grime. As he coughed and choked on the fine powder created by crushed concrete, he continued to yell for David.

"Please, God," he prayed, "help me and David!"

Lexmark Aristide

Port-au-Prince, Haiti, January 12, 2010

As the initial violent shaking stopped, Lexmark's first thought was to get to his father. But as he tried to get up, he realized he had been pinned beneath a concrete block that had fallen on his legs.

"Papa!" he cried out. The air seemed to be more dust than air, as he drew in panicked breaths.

"I am here, Lexmark," his father called from somewhere in the rubble. "I have your brother still in my arms. Are you OK?"

"I cannot move, Papa," Lexmark said, his voice tight with fear. "I am hurt." The pain from his pinned legs coursed through his entire body and pulsated in his head.

"I will find a way to get to you," his father said, determination in his voice.

"I see a light. Your brother and I will get out, and I will come for you. Do not be afraid."

Lexmark found comfort in his father's words, but he was afraid. Very afraid.

Dan Woolley

Port-au-Prince, Haiti, January 12, 2010

Somehow Dan's panic had shifted to a strange mixture of calm and dread. He knew he was in a desperate situation, but his muscles seemed to relax as his mind regained focus. He knew aftershocks were sure to follow such a big earthquake, and he needed to get to a safer place if he could.

He touched the back of his head as it throbbed and pulled his hand away. It was wet with blood.

That doesn't mean it's serious. Head wounds always bleed a lot, he thought, trying to remain calm. He reached down to his left leg, and found a large piece of concrete on top of it. He was able to heave the concrete away. He grasped blindly at the other pieces of rubble that held his foot until he had freed himself. His shoe came off in the struggle to pull his foot out of the tangled debris. He tried to pull the shoe out, but it was wedged so tightly, he gave up.

Dan felt his camera thump against his chest. He had forgotten it was there. He began to use the camera to flash a light into the blackness, to get a sense of his surroundings. He'd lost his glasses, so he couldn't see far, but he could see how close he had come to being crushed.

He flashed the light at his khakis to assess the damage to his left leg. He was shocked to see his pants soaked with blood. Putting any weight on his leg sent unbearable pain coursing through him. He worried his injury might be severe, but he knew he needed to focus on finding a safer place before an aftershock shifted the precariously balanced debris.

He crouched and took a picture under some rubble. In the tiny screen he saw the shaft of the elevators he and David had bypassed to take the open-air stairway. They both appeared intact. And miraculously, the door was open on one of them.

I need to find a way to get to that, he thought. *If everything shifts, that is the safest place I could be.*

Dan crawled through shards of broken glass, torn metal, and shattered concrete. Debris ripped into the gash in his already wounded leg. When he finally stood in the small space in front of the elevators, the pain in his injured leg made him woozy. But his relief at making it to a place where he could safely tend to his injuries fueled him with enough strength to hobble into the open shaft.

The Hotel Montana, after sustaining massive damage from the earthquake

As he leaned against the wall inside the elevator, everything began to tremble from a strong aftershock. Dan tried to steady himself, but fell to the floor. Outside, the concrete and twisted metal he had just crawled through shifted and crashed to the ground.

Evans Monsignac

Port-au-Prince, Haiti, January 12, 2010

Evans lay on the floor of the La Saline food market, pinned under concrete slabs, unable to turn his body in any direction. The dust was so thick it ground between his teeth. He had survived the initial earthquake. And an aftershock almost as big as the quake had just shifted the debris around him.

The screaming had not stopped since the first quake struck. Screams echoed through the pockets of open space under the rubble. Somewhere people prayed loudly and sang hymns.

For a few moments, he thought he had been killed. But the sound of the others crying out assured him, he was still alive. Then the pain of the concrete on top of his body settled in, leaving no doubt.

The utter and complete darkness was like nothing Evans had ever seen. He silently prayed that God would send someone to save him. He thought of his wife and 4-year-old twins, a son named Michael and a daughter named Keline. He wondered how they would get by without him.

What if they are injured? Or worse, he wondered, his stomach knotted with worry, *"what if they need me now?* Reality settled in. He could not help his wife or children. He could not even help himself.

Dan Woolley

Port-au-Prince, Haiti, January 12, 2010

Dan had forgotten his phone was in his pocket. When he pulled it out, he tried to text his wife but there was no signal. Disappointed, Dan sat down on the chunks of broken concrete. The chunks poked uncomfortably into his skin. He examined his injured leg. His flesh was split from his knee to just above his ankle, and he could see the fat under the muscle. Blood flowed from the gaping wound.

Dan couldn't recall much of his first aid training, but he had a first aid app on his phone. Luckily it didn't require an Internet connection so Dan was able to pull up information about how to treat his injury. He used his outer shirt to wrap his leg and secured the wrap with an insulated wire he ripped from the corner of the elevator.

I did not survive the earthquake to die from this leg wound, he thought, hoping it would be enough pressure to stop the bleeding.

He tried to find a way to get comfortable, but the metal box he had taken shelter in was covered in sharp, shattered concrete. Every time he moved, the suffocating dust rose into the air, making it difficult to breathe, adding a fresh layer of grit to his face and arms.

Allison Insley-Madsen
Port-au-Prince, Haiti, January 12, 2010

"Wow, that was a big one," Dr. Maggie said as she walked into the exam room shortly after the large aftershock shook the building.

"We need to get out of the building," Allison said, hugging Jack close to her. They had barely avoided being hit by breaking glass, but Maggie's assistant had pulled them away from the danger.

"No, it's over now," Dr. Maggie said calmly. "Let's get that peel off your face."

"No, we need to get home." Allison said. "I need to call my husband and make sure he's OK."

Before Dr. Maggie could protest, Allison and Jack hurried from the room. Allison pulled her phone from her purse as they got outside the building and called her husband, Eric. As she stood outside the doctor's office, waiting for Eric to pick up, she realized how bad the earthquake had actually been. Most of the buildings around her had been reduced to heaps of broken concrete and twisted metal.

"Hello!" Eric said, his voice tight with worry.

"We're OK," Allison said quickly. "Are you hurt?"

"Thank God," Eric replied. "I'm OK, too. And my parents are here with me."

Allison felt a weight of worry lifted off her. As she looked around in awe, she realized that they had been very lucky. She glanced back at the four-story building she had been inside. It seemed to be perfectly intact. Dr. Maggie's husband had designed it to withstand the potential destruction of an earthquake. His design had kept them safe.

Laura Wagner
Port-au-Prince, Haiti, January 12, 2010

Opening her eyes to the darkness that had engulfed her, Laura was surprised to still be alive. She felt her left arm crushed by the door frame she had been standing in for protection. She tried to move, but her legs were pinned under chunks of the second floor and roof that had caved in on top of her.

Beyond the rubble that buried her alive, she heard screaming and praying. Then voices began to sing. There was a strange comfort in the chaos she could hear because it meant that the world hadn't ended.

Laura was in the kitchen, which was just off her bedroom. When she felt something warm and wet on her shirt, she immediately thought some of the black bean soup called *sos pwa* they'd had for lunch had spilled on her when the refrigerator was overturned.

When I get out, I will have to tell Melise about this, Laura thought, amused to have the entire front of her shirt drenched in *sos pwa* while buried under the wreckage of the house. Melise worked at the house Laura was staying in. They had become close friends. Melise often called Laura her third daughter.

But then Laura realized the wetness on her shirt was not soup, but her own blood. And another jarring thought struck. Melise had been upstairs when the quake hit. But Laura did not hear Melise's voice among the others that sang and cried out.

Allison Insley-Madsen
Port-au-Prince, Haiti, January 12, 2010

Jack sat quietly on the floor in the back of the vehicle doing his homework. Allison hoped he would keep busy and not look at the destruction they drove past. The houses that once stood up and down the sides of the hills had crumbled into heaps.

Those who emerged from the rubble looked white and red — their skin and clothes covered in chalky dust, blood flowing from their wounds. The traffic barely moved. Debris blocked the roads and people walked around the streets confused and injured.

As their vehicle sat in traffic, Lamarre stuck his head out the window. "What do you know about the damage?" he asked.

A man turned to him, his face twisted with shock and fear, and replied, "The international hotels are destroyed. The grocery story is nothing but rubble." He turned away and continued walking.

"The grocery store," Allison breathed the words past her lips in a whisper as she glanced back at Jack. "If Dr. Maggie hadn't called, we would have been . . ."

"But you were not," Lamarre stopped her. He smiled, but distress was evident in his eyes.

"Have you reached your family?" Allison asked. She knew he had to be sick with worry.

"The phone towers must be down," he replied.

Allison looked at the injured people walking around the rubble and prayed for Lamarre's family.

Their vehicle had barely moved for three hours. Darkness settled in as they sat frozen in traffic.

"We will need to walk the rest of the way," Lamarre said.

Allison looked at the hill they would need to climb to get to her home.

"I will carry Jack," Lamarre said.

Allison nodded. "Yes, let's go."

Laura Wagner
Port-au-Prince, Haiti, January 12, 2010

"Laura! Melise! Can anybody hear me?" Laura recognized the voice of her friend, Frenel, who also worked at the home where she was staying.

"I'm here!" Laura cried. "I'm in the kitchen."

"I am coming, Lolo!" he called back, referring to her by the nickname he always used for her. "I will get you out."

She heard Frenel chipping away at the concrete. She heard him grunt as he heaved large pieces of debris to the side as he tunneled toward her through the debris. Laura wanted to help, but with her arm badly hurt, she was helpless. She couldn't see him, but she sensed he was getting closer.

"Pray, Lolo. You must pray," he told her calmly.

And so she did. She prayed and waited for two hours, trusting her friend would not stop until he reached her. Even through the aftershocks, Frenel continued to dig and chip his way through.

When Frenel finally pulled Laura through the passage he had created, she saw the small hammer in his hand, the kind typically used to hang a picture on a wall. His knuckles were bleeding.

"Thank you, Frenel," Laura said.

"You are safe!" he said, his face lit with joy. "We will get you to the United Nations compound. They will help you, Lolo."

Laura winced as Frenel helped her limp over the broken walls that had once covered her. Fenel looked down and saw that she had no shoes on.

"Here, Lolo, you wear these," he said, removing his sandals. "I will be OK." Frenel smiled and bent over, putting the sandals on Laura's feet. "We will go get you help, now."

Allison Insley-Madsen

Port-au-Prince, Haiti,
January 12, 2010, 8:30 p.m.

They walked over crumbled homes as they made their way up the hill. The suffering around them was overwhelming. Everywhere they saw the broken bodies of those who had been injured and the broken hearts of those who cried out for their loved ones. In the midst of the crying, other voices sang hymns of hope and comfort.

Now they walked through the front gate of Allison's home. The walls around their yard had fallen apart, but her home appeared to be intact. About a dozen people had taken refuge in the yard.

Allison walked cautiously into her home. Although it appeared to be in fairly good shape, she suspected it had been structurally compromised, and she also knew aftershocks would likely continue. She didn't want to become a fatality of the quakes by being inside a building when another tremor hit. But she needed to gather a few items.

Allison found her mother-in-law standing in the kitchen, wearing her nightgown. She appeared shocked and dazed. Allison was surprised to see the decorative plates on top of her cupboards unharmed. But everything that had been inside the cupboards had spilled out onto the floor, creating a mess of oils and broken glass.

"We shouldn't be in here," her mother-in-law said.

"I'll get a few things and meet you outside," Allison replied. "I'll be fast."

Allison quickly gathered her family's passports along with a few staples such as crackers, bread, peanut butter, water, batteries, and flashlights. Her home had always been her safe place. Now she took one last look around, frightened to be there. So many homes had fallen apart on top of their occupants. Safe places had become tombs in a matter of seconds.

Laura Wagner

Port-au-Prince, Haiti, January 12, 2010

Laura sat among the battered and bleeding people on the cracked concrete, clutching a metallic emergency blanket someone had handed her when she'd arrived. They were in front of the United Nations compound, which lay in a crumbled heap behind them. As the aftershocks rolled in steadily, the dazed crowd held hands and prayed.

A small boy wandered up to the group alone. Tears streaked his dust-covered face. Laura looked around to see if anyone might be with him, but he seemed to be alone. He looked at Laura, fear and confusion in his eyes. She reached her hands toward him and smiled weakly. He walked to her, and let her wrap him in her arms, then settled onto her lap. Pulling the emergency blanket over him, she held the small child as he trembled.

Lexmark had been lying under the rubble, his lower body crushed under a concrete block, for at least three hours. Thankfully, his father and baby brother had found a way out. Since then, he had been able to hear his father and their neighbors working to dig him out.

"We are very close," his father said. "Be brave."

"OK," Lexmark said, taking a deep breath, "your voice sounds close."

"Soon you will see my face," his father said.

His father's voice eased his fear. He feared all the movement above him might cause something to shift and crush him even more. He was afraid he might not make it out of the darkness in which he was trapped. He had never seen such darkness. Even on the darkest nights, his eyes could adjust. But his eyes could not adjust to this darkness. It was too absolute.

Finally, a ray of light broke through the rubble. And then more light. He shut his eyes against the shock of brightness. When he looked again, his father was looking down at him. Sweat streaked his father's dusty face and a smile rose to his cheeks. Lexmark smiled back, despite the pain in his legs. He knew for certain now that he would soon be free.

Dan Woolley

Port-au-Prince, Haiti, January 12, 2010

Throughout the hours he had been trapped, Dan would occasionally hear voices calling out for help. He decided to try to make contact with them.

"Help!" he screamed. "I'm injured."

"We're over here," a man replied. His voice was deep and strong and cut through the debris more clearly than any other voices. "Can you help us?"

"I'm in the elevator." Dan said. "Where are you?"

The voice faded in and out, but Dan heard something about the lobby and the front desk.

"There are five of us, trapped in a pocket that's only 3 feet tall . . . worried we might run out of air," the man said. "Is anyone else with you?"

"No, I'm alone," Dan replied.

"Can you move around?" the man asked.

"It's not really safe for me to leave," Dan replied.

There was nothing he could do. No place for him to go. Just a few hours ago, they had all been standing in the lobby. If the man had called out to him then, Dan could have simply walked to him. Now they were so close, yet impossibly separated.

Dan learned the man talking to him was Jim Gulley. With him were Rick, Ann, Clint, and Sam. Clint and Sam had been pinned by debris. All five of them were relief workers from the United States. Another woman, Sarla, was trapped near them. She was able to move around a bit, and was trying desperately to find a hole in the rubble.

Now Dan felt a greater sense of how truly desperate his situation was. He tried not to think about running out of air.

Then Dan heard a scraping sound. Hoping it might be a rescuer, Dan asked, "Can you help us?"

"No," replied a voice with a Haitian accent.

"Are you trapped?" Dan asked.

"Yes," the man replied.

The man, Lukeson, was trapped in the elevator shaft beside Dan. Lukeson had been trying to climb out, hoping to get into Dan's shaft. But the walls of the elevator were simply too high to climb over.

While it was frustrating to know people were so nearby, but unable to see or touch one another, Dan found comfort in knowing he wasn't completely alone.

Allison Insley-Madsen
Port-au-Prince, Haiti, January 12, 2010

Even though the air was quite warm, Allison's body quivered. She knew this was a normal symptom of shock. Despite what she had seen with her own eyes — despite knowing it was all really happening — it was difficult to believe she wasn't stuck inside a terrible nightmare.

Her family was preparing to spend the night in the yard. They had pulled mattresses from the house, and tried to rest as the aftershocks continued.

Many people still sang and prayed. Much like the aftershocks and the sounds of more buildings collapsing, the singing never stopped.

Something inside the house jingled. This had become a signal that an aftershock was coming. She braced herself. Jack, who was lying beside her, reached over and took her hand. She squeezed his small fist and kissed his forehead reassuringly.

As the earth began to tremble again, somewhere in the distance the terrible collision of concrete falling down thundered into the darkness. And again the songs of hope and faith rose up to follow the crash, as if to chase the echoes of destruction away.

Earthquake survivors were forced to sleep outside due to lack of shelter and the threat of aftershocks.

51

PRAYERS IN THE DARKNESS

4

A rescuer works to free an earthquake survivor who is trapped beneath rubble.

Dan Woolley

Port-au-Prince, Haiti,
January 13, 2010

In the total darkness, Dan retreated into his thoughts. He also prayed, talked with Lukeson and Jim, and made an occasional joke with them. He even sang out a few hymns. All of these things reminded him he was alive.

His phone still had power, but he wanted to preserve it as much as possible. He checked the time. It was just before midnight.

"Dan, how are you and Lukeson doing?" Jim yelled from the lobby.

"Lukeson, how are you?" Dan asked.

"I am fine, Daniel," Lukeson replied.

Dan yelled back to Jim, letting him know they were both OK.

Then Dan was back in his own thoughts. He thought about his wife, Christy, and their sons, Josh and Nathan. He knew they would be very worried about him. He wished desperately to have just one more conversation with his family.

He found a journal he'd been carrying in his pants pocket. Luckily, he still had a couple of pens as well. He used the camera to get a quick glimpse of the opened journal. Using this flash

method, he found a page, and then began writing.
Unable to see his own words, he used his thumb as a
guide to space the lines apart as best he could.

If found, please give to my wife, Christina.

I love you.

I love Josh and Nathan, the joy and pride of my life.

He tried to tell them everything he wanted them
to know about his love for them. He tried to give
them his deepest hopes for their futures and the
fatherly advice he hoped he could give them face to
face if he survived.

. . . Don't just live. Change the world!

Dan took a break from writing. He had been
trapped for many hours and he felt terribly thirsty.
He thought of a survival show he'd seen on TV
warning that people could die of dehydration in just
three days.

He struggled to find a way to rest comfortably
enough to fall asleep. As he lay back trying to relax,
he felt pressure in his bladder letting him know he
needed to urinate. The survival show's host had
said drinking your own urine could help you survive
longer without water. When he'd watched the show,

the idea had made him squeamish, but now he was willing to try.

The only trouble was he didn't have anything to urinate into. He took off his T-shirt, cupped it in his hands, and used it like a sponge to absorb the liquid so he could wring it into his mouth. It tasted as terrible as he'd imagined, but the fact that he was taking steps to survive also gave him hope.

He hung his wet shirt over a handrail to dry out. The concrete rubbed against his bare skin as he lay down, and though he was in a tropical region, the air made him shiver. After an hour of shivering, he decided he'd be more comfortable with his damp shirt on. With his shirt back on, he closed his eyes, hoping he could sleep at least a couple of hours.

Rosemary Pierre
Port-au-Prince, Haiti, January 13, 2010

Many families had come to the school immediately after the quake. So many people called out the names of their loved ones who had entered the school that afternoon.

The women sang hymns and prayed, their cheeks streaked with tears. Many had worked through the night, Rosemary and her aunt Josette included. Rosemary stumbled as she hefted a large piece of concrete to the side, her thin body quivering under the weight. The thought of finding Stephanie alive fueled Rosemary just enough to keep her searching through her exhaustion. But Rosemary feared her cousin lay crushed beneath the concrete.

"You are wearing yourself out. You should take a break," Josette said gently.

There had been a tapping from somewhere below, and several of those who had gathered were desperately creating a tunnel through the debris.

"You have been working all night, Rosemary," Romules said. "Go rest for a bit. I will keep digging."

Reluctantly, Rosemary stepped down from the heap that had once been her school. Josette hugged her. Rosemary's shoulders shook as she began to sob. She had been so focused on finding Stephanie that she had not let herself cry.

"We will come back. We will not stop until we find her," Josette said firmly.

"Where will we rest?" Rosemary asked, looking at Josette through tears. "We have no home. We have no place to even lie down."

There was so much uncertainty as Rosemary thought of her family and friends. Who had survived? Who was now buried alive and hurt? The realization that there were likely many people she cared about whom she would never see again made her chest ache with sadness.

Josette looked around solemnly. "We will rest here." She sat in the dirt and motioned for Rosemary to join her. Rosemary curled up on the hard ground, rested her head on her aunt's lap, and closed her eyes.

Allison Insley-Madsen

Port-au-Prince, Haiti, January 13, 2010

After waking up from a restless night of sleep, Allison walked into her front yard and saw that about 30 people had settled there, many of them seriously injured.

Wiping away tears, she took a deep breath and gathered her strength. She found a neighbor woman, a local police chief, who had suffered a severe injury to her head.

"My children did not get out of the house," the woman said, crying. "I pray for a miracle, but when I call to them, there is no answer."

"I'm so sorry," Allison said.

"Our dog was trapped under the concrete. He cried all night. Until a kind man asked if he could put him out of his misery." She wiped her tears, then looked up at Allison. "My children do not cry. I pray that means they do not feel pain or fear."

A man carrying a small black doctor's bag stopped beside them and looked at the woman's injured head.

"May I treat your injury?" he asked.

Allison watched him quietly clean the wound, then gazed at the crowd of injured people. So many needed medical attention. Earlier, Allison had walked past the local hospital and saw how devastated it had been by the quake. Under the circumstances, this man's little bag of supplies might be the only hope of medical care they had.

Dan's thoughts returned to his friend David, who had been standing so close to him when the earthquake struck. He'd hoped David had just been knocked unconscious.

Occasionally through the night, Dan had heard Jim helping guide Sarla as she tried to find her way through the rubble, searching for a small crack where she could see light. She was the only one in a position to move around in the debris, but it was dangerous, and she was moving in the same utter darkness that blinded Dan where he was trapped.

When he heard the sound of helicopter blades cutting through the sky, he called out to Lukeson, "Did you hear that?"

"Helicopters!" Lukeson called back.

"Sarla sees some light," Jim shouted. "She's not able to get to it, but we're trying to figure out a way she can get there safely."

Dan told Lukeson about Sarla and the light. The extra distance and barriers between them was just enough to make it difficult for Lukeson to hear Jim. While he relayed the information, Dan allowed himself to feel hopeful. But he also knew it could mean very little. Even if Sarla got someone's attention, how would rescuers ever get to them through six stories of concrete rubble?

While Sarla continued to struggle toward the light, Dan could hear Jim encouraging her and calling out updates on her progress. Dan would then share the information with Lukeson.

Dan was beginning to doubt Sarla could make it, but then Jim reported that she had actually gotten to the light. Dan could hear her yelling, but her voice sounded so quiet, he wondered if anyone above would ever hear her. Just then, Jim shouted some encouraging news.

"She made contact with someone. He is speaking Creole, so she cannot understand him. Ann and I spoke to him in French, and he said, 'OK' — then we heard him leave. We believe he's going to get help."

Allison stood in front of a pot of stew she had thrown together with items from her kitchen. It wasn't the most appetizing meal, but it was all she could offer.

"Please tell everyone to bring a bowl or a cup to get some stew," she said to her maid.

Her maid nodded and hurried to the crowd gathered in the yard. After a few moments, the woman returned.

"They do not have bowls or cups. They have nothing," she said.

Allison grabbed a ream of tin foil and ripped a sheet off. "Then we'll have to make bowls," she said.

Hours had passed since Sarla had made contact. Yet no one had returned for them.

"Maybe they can't find her location?" Dan called out to Jim. "Perhaps we should start banging again?"

Jim said, "Here we go! One, two, three. HELP!"

Dan screamed with them and used a chunk of concrete to bang against the elevator.

It felt like no one was ever going to come back for them. Dan decided to use a bit of phone battery to write a few last messages to his family.

I think I will likely pass to heaven tonight or tomorrow. The rescuers have not returned — likely too difficult a rescue and too many other, easier needs.

If I die know that I fell asleep without pain.

That last sentence was not entirely true. He was in pain, but it wasn't agonizing. He didn't want his wife to be left with an image of him in agony.

I will always love you.

"President Préval, what are you doing here at the airport?" Dr. Sanjay Gupta, reporting for CNN, held a microphone toward the shocked president of Haiti. The severely damaged airport loomed behind them.

"My palace collapsed," he replied wearily.

"So you don't have a home?" Gupta asked.

"I came here to work, but they told me I cannot work here because it is not safe. I cannot live in the palace. I cannot live in my own house because the two collapsed," he replied.

"Where will you go tonight?"

"I don't know," he replied, dragging his hand over his face as if trying to wipe some of the stress away.

"It's striking, the president of this country doesn't know where he's going to sleep tonight," Gupta noted.

"I have plenty of time to look for a bed. But for now, I am looking for a way to rescue the people," President Préval replied.

There were so many injured, and many more buried alive. It had been nearly two days since the quake struck. He was exhausted and had not slept. The horror of the situation was truly overwhelming.

René Préval

The sounds of airplanes filled the night sky as Allison and her family spent another night outside. Exhausted, Jack had curled up and fallen asleep between her and her husband, Eric.

"Tomorrow, we are going to the airport to get on a plane to go back to the U.S.," she said.

"Yes," Eric agreed. "You take Jack and my father."

Eric's father had been in poor health, so they thought it best for him to go with Allison and for Eric to stay behind to get the family business back up and running. The bottled water their company produced would be greatly needed in the days to come. Another facet of their business involved port and airport operations, which would also be important to help bring supplies into the country.

Eric's mother wanted to begin cleaning up and rebuilding her home. Leaving her husband and mother-in-law behind worried Allison, but she knew it was the plan that made the most sense.

IN THE RUBBLE

5

A volunteer Haitian rescue team searches for survivors
in the collapsed remains of a building.

Rosemary Pierre

Port-au-Prince, Haiti, January 14, 2010

Rosemary stood in front of the rubble of the
school where her cousin Stephanie had been
buried. Despite the hours of calling her name
and digging through the rubble alongside others
searching for their loved ones for the past two

days, they had not found her. They had heaved and pushed the heavy concrete chunks until the skin on their knuckles had been rubbed away and the gray slabs were speckled red with blood.

The many bodies that had been pulled from the rubble were laid out along the side of the road. Each time another lifeless form was carried away from the debris, Rosemary looked to see if it was Stephanie. Many were her friends. Her heart broke again with each familiar face she saw. But she continued to hope that her cousin might still be alive. The mixture of sorrow and hope was emotionally exhausting.

Josette had left briefly to find some food and water. But she had returned with nothing. A woman searching for her son shared a few crackers with them. And someone had given them a single bottle of water to share. Rosemary's stomach ached with hunger. Her head throbbed from dehydration.

As far as she knew there had been no communication from President Préval or any governmental leaders. No one had a radio to hear whatever news there might be. They could hear the planes flying in and hoped that meant help was coming.

Rosemary saw a truck rumble down the road and stop a few yards away from the destroyed school. United Nations soldiers emerged, and several survivors hurried toward them.

"They have come with food and water," one woman called out.

Josette and Rosemary joined the crowd that flocked to the truck. A few soldiers worked to organize the desperate people who quickly gathered. There were so many of them, ravaged by hunger and thirst, standing weakly in front of the truck. Rosemary prayed there would be enough food and water.

The screams of those trapped around Evans had stopped. And the smell of the decaying dead had begun to fill the hot air inside the pocket within which Evans was hopelessly pinned. He could hear others walking around the rubble above, occasionally calling out names. In such complete darkness and fading in and out of consciousness, he lost all sense of time. He guessed he had been trapped beneath the slabs of concrete for at least two nights.

He ached with hunger. He worried if he didn't get something in his stomach, he could die from dehydration or eventually starve to death.

He had noticed something wet flowing beneath him. He struggled to twist his body, cupped his hands in the liquid, then pulled his cupped hands to his lips. The smell was awful, but he was so thirsty. He took a small sip, then immediately wretched and gagged. After a moment, he scooped another handful of the foul liquid.

He could hear rescuers working around the devastated market. He held onto hope that he would be found alive. If drinking sewage was the only way to keep from starving or dehydrating, he would do it.

Lexmark Aristide

Fond Parisien, Haiti, January 14, 2010

After Lexmark was pulled safely from the rubble, he was taken, along with his father and baby brother, to the border town of Fond Parisien, where he was given life-saving treatment for the severe injuries he had sustained when his lower body was crushed.

Lexmark, wearing a full pelvic cast, lay beside his father. "Where will we go when I am better?" he asked.

"I am not sure," his father replied.

"We have nothing because everything we had has been destroyed."

"But we have our family," Lexmark said.

"God will help us with the rest," his father said.

Allison Insley-Madsen

Allison, her son, Jack, and her father-in-law sat in a car traveling toward the airport. The large pieces of debris that littered the streets made the roads difficult to pass through. The vibrantly colored walls of buildings that had once lined the streets were now reduced to piles of gray and beige rubble. Piled on each corner of the road were bodies that had been recovered from the debris.

"I can't wait to see what you're building, Jack," she said quietly to her son. He kept his head down, focused on the building blocks she had grabbed from the house before they left. She hoped they would keep his attention focused away from the destruction and death that surrounded them. Other than that one set of toys, they were leaving with only the clothes on their backs.

"It's going to be really big, Mommy," Jack replied as he clicked another block into place.

Allison glanced back toward the hill upon which her house sat. Her house was the only building still standing.

Bill Clinton

Harlem, New York, January 14, 2010

Former President Bill Clinton sat in his office with 50 philanthropists discussing how they could help Haiti. Clinton had felt a special connection to Haiti since he and his wife, Hillary, now secretary of state in President Barack Obama's administration, first visited the island nation on their honeymoon in 1975.

He had been shocked by the news of the earthquake and the ongoing reports of devastation in the city of Port-au-Prince. So many people, including friends of his, were injured and unaccounted for. This was more than just a terrible disaster that happened in another country. This was deeply personal to Clinton, and he intended to help in whatever way he could.

Now his office had emptied out, and Clinton sat at his computer typing the final words of an article for *Time* magazine.

"Before this disaster, Haiti had the best chance in my lifetime to fulfill its potential as a country to basically escape the chains of the past 200 years. I still believe that if we rally around them now and support them in the right way, the Haitian people can reclaim their destiny."

Allison Insley-Madsen

Port-au-Prince, Haiti, January 14, 2010

As they stood in front of the badly damaged airport, Allison heard someone call out to her.

"Allison!"

"Don," she replied, recognizing the man who had been her boss at the U.S. embassy in Paris. "I can't tell you how great it is to see you. We're trying to get back to the U.S."

"Well, you've come to the right place," he said, smiling. "We'll get you there. Come with me."

As they walked briskly through the airport, which looked like it was on the verge of collapsing, Allison was unnerved by the eerie emptiness of the building, which appeared to be completely deserted. As they emerged behind the building, she saw two members of the U.S. Air Force seated at a card table, providing makeshift air traffic control for the airport because the tower had been destroyed. She understood from her training that these men were coordinating planes from all over the world as they came to Haiti to deliver aid and rescue foreign citizens.

So many planes with relief supplies were crammed into a small space, and many more waited for clearance to land. It was good to see the international response, but even with the help coming in, Allison knew the time ahead for Haiti would be nightmarish. While she felt blessed to be able to return to the United States, her heart sank as she thought of her friends who had no choice but to stay.

When Jim announced that Sarla had found a
new opening and was able to see a tree and a beam
of light from a helicopter, Dan's senses seemed to
spring back to life. Sarla's voice sounded weak as
she called out for help.

"Jim, let's all yell again," Dan suggested.

Jim counted off, and they all began pounding
and screaming for help. When they stopped,
gasping for breath, they sat silently and listened.
Still no one responded.

"Sarla can see a person near her, but they
cannot hear her," Jim said.

Dan's heart was racing. He felt so helpless and
frustrated knowing people were so close but still
unable to hear their cries for help. Then he heard
Sarla talking but couldn't make out what she was
saying. He waited anxiously for an update from
Jim. Before he got one, he heard Jim passing
along information that Dan and Lukeson were
trapped nearby.

Finally, Jim called out to Dan. "Sarla made contact with a French rescue team! They've asked for all of our names and a summary of our injuries. They've gone to get equipment to rescue us and promised to come right back!"

Dan pumped his fist into the air and whooped for joy. Then he joined Jim and the others in singing a song of praise to God.

"Daniel, what's going on?" Lukeson asked.

In his joy, Dan had forgotten to tell Lukeson what was going on. He quickly filled him in.

"That's good. Very good news," Lukeson replied, his voice weak and shaky.

The sound of Lukeson's voice worried Dan. "Hang in there, Lukeson. It's only a matter of hours how."

Allison Insley-Madsen
Port-au-Prince, Haiti, January 14, 2010

It had been such a long day. Planes came and went, and they had waited for more than eight hours for one that could take them to Santo Domingo in the Dominican Republic. From there, they would be able to return to the United States. Now their wait was nearly over.

Don made sure they each had a packaged military meal called an MRE for dinner. By the time they boarded the plane shortly after 8:00 p.m., Jack could barely keep his eyes open. Giving up his seat so that one more person could fit on the flight, Jack curled up on duffel bags between seats and was asleep almost as soon as they got into the air.

Twenty minutes after takeoff, they landed at the Santo Domingo airport. In less than an hour, they traveled to a hotel, took their first shower in three days, and put on fresh clothes.

Allison lay beside Jack in the hotel bed thinking about the sounds of agony and grief that had been their constant chorus the past three days. Although she was physically removed from it all, her mind clung to the sights, sounds, and smells. Sometimes she thought that the earth was trembling beneath them, but it seemed her mind was simply playing tricks on her.

She told herself over and over again that it was just a psychological effect of the post-traumatic stress she was likely suffering from. She kept reminding herself that she was safe and the earth was not moving. Finally, exhaustion pulled her into a deep sleep.

Dan Woolley

Port-au-Prince, Haiti,
January 15, 2010, 1:00 a.m.

Late Thursday night, the French rescue team had reached Sarla. She led them to Jim and the others, and by midnight they were working to free the five trapped people. Before Jim was removed, he called out to Dan. He said that Ann was staying to translate for the rescuers as they worked to free Clint and Sam.

"They know about you and Lukeson. We'll remind them to come for you."

"Thank you, Jim!" Dan replied.

That was hours ago. And still no one had returned for Dan and Lukeson. Dan had grown increasingly worried about Lukeson. Each time Dan spoke to him, it seemed that Lukeson had grown weaker.

A woman with the French rescue team had spoken with Dan and assured him they had not forgotten him and Lukeson. But then that group of rescuers had been replaced with another that continued to work on freeing the pinned men.

Then everything had gone silent for hours.

Maybe they took a break to regroup. Maybe they had to get more equipment to get to us, Dan reasoned. *Maybe, in the chaos, they forgot about us.*

Dan and Lukeson began banging and yelling for help. But no one seemed to hear them. Then, finally, Dan heard an American voice acknowledge them.

"I've got two new contacts here," said the voice. "My crew can't get to them. I need a new crew!"

The words startled and angered Dan. "We're not new! We're on a list!" He paused, hoping they would respond, but there was only silence. "Please, don't forget us!"

Dan could hear rescuers above him. Many voices in many different languages. He could imagine the confusion as various teams searched for survivors. He also realized that rescuing him and Lukeson might simply be too difficult. If there were other survivors that were easier to access, he assumed the rescue teams would get them out first. But the thought that he might die surrounded by rescuers caused panic to rise up inside him.

He began banging and yelling desperately until he ran out of strength and crumpled to the elevator floor out of breath. His phone was almost out of power, but he quickly checked the time. It was 3:15 a.m. Nearly two-and-a-half hours had passed since the French team removed the last of Jim's group. There was no doubt in Dan's mind that he and Lukeson had been forgotten by that team of rescuers. And now he worried the new teams above him might never reach them.

Dan's heart raced. His body began to shake as his shallow breaths came rapidly. His shirt was drenched in sweat. He prayed, trying to slow his breathing. Then he began to sing songs of worship. He visualized himself lying in a field, watching clouds pass over him. He prayed and sang and accepted that it might be God's will that he not survive.

Then he heard a voice call out to him. "Hello. Is anybody there?"

"Yes! Yes! I'm here. I'm here!" Dan yelled back. The rescuer said that his name was Sam and he was in the elevator shaft trying to make his way to Dan, but it was difficult. Dan could hear the buzz of saws cutting through concrete. They were coming for him!

After a while he heard a man ask Sam, "What are you doing?"

"I'm working toward the guys in the elevator," Sam replied.

The other man said some words that were too muffled for Dan to make out, and then he said something Dan heard very clearly. "We can't afford to spend our time on that right now. Our shift's almost over." More muffled words followed. Then an angry shout, "You're on your own time, then!"

Dan became desperate. He banged and yelled every few minutes. They couldn't forget him again. He had to get free. He could hear voices speaking in many different languages. Saws continued to buzz. He yelled and screamed and banged.

"Hey, we're in the elevator shaft. Help us! We're injured! Can you hear me?"

"Quiet!" an American voice called back harshly.

"There are two of us," Dan continued yelling. "We're in the elevators!"

"We can't get to you," the voice replied gruffly. Then the men above him continued talking to one another about changing bits and getting another saw.

Dan would not leave it at that. He refused to accept that they could not get him. He screamed louder. "Do you hear me? Are you listening?" Lukeson joined him and began calling out phrases in other languages.

"Be quiet! Be quiet!" someone yelled.

But Dan refused to be quiet. He only yelled louder. But no one would respond to him. And then someone finally did.

"We're not coming for you. We're not going to rescue you! Shut up!"

Trapped between a portion of the grocery store's concrete ceiling and wall, Wismond could only move his upper body. With four stories of concrete on top of him, he wondered if anyone would ever find him, but he held onto hope as he prayed.

"Dear God, please save me from this." He spoke the words aloud, the sound of his own voice a comfort in the thick blackness. For a while there had been crying and screaming that seemed to be coming from under the rubble not far from him. Now he heard only the muffled voices of people searching for survivors and the sound of helicopters flying above.

He could hear hymns being sung from beyond the rubble. He recited psalms as he drifted in and out of sleep. The words lifted his spirits despite the hopelessness of his situation. Periodically, he would bang on the broken walls that held him captive, hoping someone above would hear him.

If only my cell phone were charged, he thought, gripping it in his hand. *Maybe then I could call someone so they would know to come find me.*

Wismond pulled the tab on another can of soda. The sound of the seal being broken echoed dully off the concrete. He took a drink, allowing the carbonated beverage to swish around his mouth, clearing the concrete dust from his teeth and tongue. He pulled another biscuit from one of the nearby packages and took a bite. He knew he was lucky to have food and drink within reach. Still, he tried his best to ration his supplies, hoping there would be enough to keep him alive until help came.

Volunteer rescuers used any tools they could find to remove rubble and help trapped survivors.

RESCUED

6

A rescue team digs into the ruins of the Hotel Montana, trying to locate survivors.

Dan Woolley

Port-au-Prince, Haiti, January 15, 2010

Dan continued to yell until another rescuer finally told him he was coming for him. But then his supervisor told him they couldn't devote all their resources to only two people. And so they never came. Dan had given up all hope, but then someone called his name.

"Dan. Dan! Can you hear me?"

"Yes," replied Dan. He recognized the voice, but wasn't sure to whom it belonged.

"Dan, I'm coming to get you!" the voice said. And then Dan realized it was Sam, the rescuer who had told Dan he was trying to get to him before his supervisor told him to stop. It had been an hour, maybe two, maybe more — Dan no longer had any sense of time — and he had given up on Sam returning for him. Yet here he was.

"I'm coming through the elevator shaft, and I'll be down there in just a minute," Sam said.

Then a man came through the shaft above him, his headlamp cutting through the darkness like a beacon of salvation. Dan's heart raced as Sam dropped to the ground in front of him and handed him a bottle of water and a flashlight.

Sam quickly assessed Dan's injuries and wrapped his wounded leg in bandages.

"Lukeson, Sam is here to rescue us!" Dan called to his friend. As he shined the light toward the wall between their elevators, he saw Lukeson wiggling his fingers through a crack. Sam was able to pass a bottle of water through the crack to him.

Sam still had to figure out some things in order to extract them. While he worked with his crew, he was able to get Dan's wife's name and number so they could let her know they were working to rescue him. Dan felt relieved, knowing how worried his wife must be.

It would take another five hours to cut a hole large enough to remove Dan and Lukeson, so they agreed it would be best, despite the danger, to pull them up the way Sam had come down, through the shaft. The shaft rose straight up several stories, then turned abruptly. Metal spikes protruded from busted concrete lining the narrow passage.

Lukeson went first. And 20 minutes later, Sam was strapping Dan into a harness. Before the rescue crew pulled him up, Dan asked Sam to please look for any sign of David. Sam agreed to look for his friend.

"And it's not a big deal, but could you look for my backpack?"

Sam promised he would do both.

As Dan was pulled through the passage, he had to use a considerable amount of what little strength he had left to maneuver himself. Along the way, eight to ten rescuers were perched on concrete corners and hung off crevices of the broken shaft. Each seemed genuinely happy to see Dan. They smiled and encouraged him the entire way, helping to reposition him so he would not be cut by debris.

It was a long, slow rise, but eventually, sunlight touched his face and warmed his battered body. Medics began working on his leg immediately while photographers and journalists swarmed around them. Then a tall, thin Haitian man walked toward Dan. He looked straight into Dan's eyes, and his smile grew wider as he got closer. He bent down and put his hand on Dan's face.

"Hello, Daniel!"

"Lukeson! I'm so glad to meet you, man!"

Finally, the two men who had been trapped side by side, separated by a metal wall for 65 hours, were able to look at each other's faces.

Dan was loaded into a van on a stretcher. As the doors were being shut, a man called out, "Wait!" Sam stepped into the van and held up Dan's backpack.

"Look what I found."

Dan smiled. After such an ordeal, getting his backpack back seemed trivial, but it brought Dan a sense of comfort he couldn't explain.

"Thank you," Dan said, shaking Sam's hand. He looked at the mud-streaked face of the young man who had just risked his life to save two others. He wondered if Sam's family and community knew that an amazing hero lived among them.

Réne Préval

Port-au-Prince, Haiti, January 15, 2010

The president and his government advisors had set up office in a local police station. President Préval had been on the phone with UN Secretary General Ban Ki-Moon, who vowed to continue sending aid to Haiti.

He had given the U.S. government temporary control of the airport, in the hope that they could get aid to those in need more quickly. Aircraft from around the world came in each day, delivering tents, blankets, food, water, and medical supplies.

Now Préval was finishing a phone call with U.S. president Barack Obama.

"I am so sorry for this tragedy," Obama said. "We promise to do all we can to help you now and long term."

"Thank you very much," Préval replied, his voice thick with exhaustion. "Please tell the American people, from the bottom of my heart and on behalf of the people of Haiti, thank you, thank you, thank you."

Rosemary and Josette had spent two nights trying to sleep on the street among dozens of others. So many had no place to call home anymore. Even those whose houses were not completely destroyed were too fearful to go inside, frightened that aftershocks could send the buildings crumbling down.

They had heard no word from the government. It felt as if the quake had shattered Haiti's leadership as well as its buildings.

"Where is our president? Why does no one tell us what we are to do?" a man cried out in frustration.

Rumors circulated that the governmental buildings had been destroyed, and that President Préval was alive and working from a police station. Rosemary had seen foreign soldiers come through with supplies and encouragement. The soldiers instructed them to go to one of the displacement camps that had sprung up around the city. There they could set up a temporary shelter.

"We must go get a tent," Josette said wearily.

"I cannot leave until we find Stephanie," Rosemary replied, her voice tight with sadness.

Josette put her hand gently on Rosemary's arm. "Stephanie would want us to take care of ourselves, as well."

Rosemary looked at the heap of concrete and twisted metal that had once been her school. Foreign rescue teams had started working on the site, using tools to break through the concrete.

Rosemary looked back at her aunt. She looked weak and worn, as if she might fall over from exhaustion and stress. She needed rest.

"I will come back as soon as we are settled," Rosemary said, reluctantly. She knew Josette was right. The two began to walk toward the nearest camp.

As they walked, Rosemary worried about her future. She had begun to accept they would likely not find Stephanie alive. She wondered how long they would have to live in tents and if the other missing members of her family would ever be found. She worried that all her own hopes for graduating and going on to college might never be a reality now that her school had been destroyed.

Her present situation was terrifying, and her future was completely uncertain. She took her aunt's hand as they walked and tried to put her worries aside. Instead she focused simply on putting one foot in front of the other as they walked slowly toward the camp.

Allison Insley-Madsen
Santo Domingo, Dominican Republic, January 15, 2010

Allison sat in the airplane with Jack in the seat beside her. They were able to get on an earlier flight than her father-in-law, but he would be coming on another plane very soon.

"It shouldn't be long before we land in Atlanta," Allison told Jack. "Just one more flight."

"I like flying. And this time I get my own seat," Jack said, smiling, as he latched his seat belt.

Allison smiled back at him. He knew the earth had shaken violently and many buildings and homes had crashed down. He had seen the injured people in their yard, heard the sadness that surrounded him. There was nothing she could do to shield him from all of that, although she tried to shield him as much as she could. But Jack had been very brave. In a way, he had made her brave, too.

Allison put her arm around Jack's shoulders and kissed the top of his head.

Bill Clinton

Washington, D.C., January 16, 2010

Standing side by side in the Rose Garden outside the Capitol building, former Presidents Bill Clinton and George W. Bush listened as President Obama stood at the podium and addressed reporters.

"We just met in the Oval Office — an office they both know well," President Obama began. "When I called each of them after I heard the tragic news of the earthquake that has devastated Haiti's capital city, they each asked the same simple question: 'How can I help?'"

He looked at the reporters and continued. "At this moment, we're moving forward with one of the largest relief efforts in our history — to save lives and to deliver relief that averts an even larger catastrophe."

As Obama stepped away from the podium, Bush took his place. He mentioned that many people wanted to send humanitarian aid such as blankets and water. "Like other relief organizations are saying, we ask that you just send cash. We promise to make sure the money is used wisely."

Clinton hoped they could make a difference for the people of Haiti that would be more than recovery and relief, but would raise the country to a place of true hope and security.

Bill Clinton
Port-au-Prince, Haiti, January 18, 2010

Bill Clinton stepped off the airplane and looked at the severely damaged airport before him, taking in his first glimpse of the devastation caused by the quake. He knew he would see much destruction as the day progressed. He also understood it was the human devastation that would affect him most.

His focus now was making sure those in need got the assistance they required to survive. He planned to help unload planes coming into the country with much-needed supplies. He would also confer with the military and hold a press conference. But he knew in his heart that true success would mean helping Haiti thrive as an independent nation. This had been his dream for helping this country since the first time he visited. And he vowed to do all he could to make it a reality.

A survivor is rescued from the rubble after being trapped for several days.

THE LAST SURVIVORS

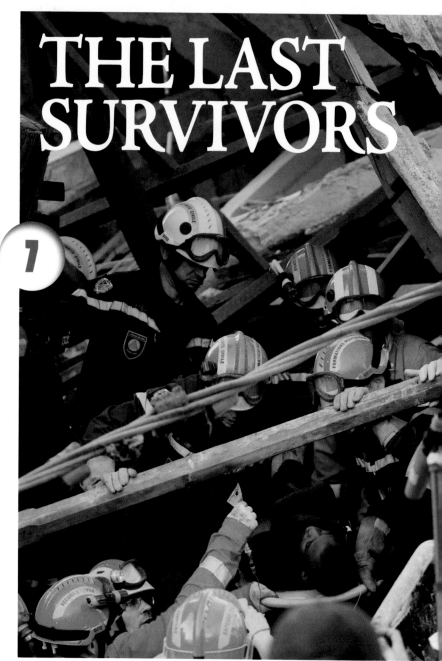

1

An international rescue team carefully pulls Wismond Exantus from the rubble on a stretcher.

Wismond Exantus

Port-au-Prince, Haiti,
January 23, 2010

Wismond heard voices above him again. He wasn't sure how many days he had been pounding at the concrete. Time had no meaning beneath the rubble. But as long as he could move, he vowed to keep trying to get someone's attention.

"Please, God, let them hear me," he prayed, not confident his tapping could be heard through the layers of rubble.

Then he heard more voices. They sounded excited but at first he couldn't quite make out what they were saying. The sound of concrete scraping against concrete drowned out the voices for a few moments. Then the voices began calling out again. This time, Wismond understood what they were saying, and he recognized the voice of his brother.

"We hear you!" his brother called out. "We are going to get help!"

Tears of joy began to flow from Wismond's eyes. "*Mesi!*" he called back. "Praise you, God, you have sent my brother to save me."

Hours passed, but the sound of rubble being cleared away never stopped. Voices called out in languages he didn't understand, while others spoke to him in Haitian Creole.

Then a light broke through into the darkness. Wismond's heart began to pound with excitement. It wasn't long before a woman slipped through a small hole the rescuers had created.

Overjoyed, Wismond smiled at the woman. She smiled back and handed him a bottle of water.

She called up the tunnel to her rescue crew above. Wismond could not understand what she was saying. But he kept smiling at every word she spoke and repeatedly spoke one word in response: "*Mesi.*" Thank you.

Days and nights seemed to blend together seamlessly under the darkened shroud of rubble, and Evans lost all sense of time as he struggled to survive by sipping handfuls of sewage as it trickled past him.

Unable to move one way or the other because of the concrete slabs pinning him to the ground, he could do nothing but lie on his back, drifting in and out of consciousness. The stench of decay stung his nostrils every time he awoke. He prayed over and over that God would save him and spare him the death that was literally all around him.

When the debris above him began to move, Evans was too weak to alert anyone that he was there, still alive. A sliver of light crept into his black tomb. Evans blinked against the brightness, as a man began to yell.

"Dear God, he is alive!" the man's voice cracked with excitement.

I am not going to die, Evans thought. *I will be free.*

EPILOGUE

The death toll of an earthquake is not only determined by the severity of the quake. The place that is struck by an earthquake also matters a great deal. In wealthier countries, structures are more likely to have been constructed to withstand earthquakes. As a result, even strong quakes will generally cause fewer deaths and injuries in these countries. When an earthquake with a magnitude of 8.8 on the Richter scale hit Chile on February 27, 2010, fewer than 550 people were killed and about 12,000 were injured.

By comparison, the earthquake that struck Haiti on January 12, 2010, registered as a magnitude 7 on the Richter scale. At least 59 aftershocks with magnitudes of 4.5 or greater followed the initial quake. An estimated 316,000 people lost their lives and another 300,000 were injured.

With the epicenter just 15 miles (24 km) west of Port-au-Prince, the government was left utterly crippled. Many nations stepped in to help with relief.

Rescue teams joined Haitians in the massive task of finding and recovering survivors from an estimated 100,000 destroyed homes and buildings.

In the weeks following the earthquake, more than 1.5 million people took up residence in the 1,556 temporary displacement camps. Three years after the quake, in January of 2013, it was reported that nearly 150,000 people continued to live in 271 remaining camps. Five years after the earthquake, tens of thousands of people remained homeless.

An earthquake survival camp in Port-au-Prince with an estimated population of 50,000 people, January 21, 2010.

Dan Woolley eventually returned home and resumed his nonprofit work. He wrote a book about his experience, titled *Unshaken: Rising from the Ruins of Haiti's Hotel Montana*. Dan continues to stay in touch with Lukeson and Jim, the man across the lobby under the wreckage.

Wismond Exantus was rescued after being buried alive for 11 days. He was treated for various injuries, malnutrition, and dehydration.

In the years following the disaster, Allison Insely-Madsen continued her volunteer work in Haiti with a therapy program for disabled children.

Lexmark Aristide and his father and brother were reunited with his mother, who also survived the earthquake. Like so many others, the family lost all their worldly possessions. Lexmark plans to finish school and become an engineer.

Laura Wagner went on to finish her PhD and spends time in Haiti helping develop Creole-language educational videos for patients who have been newly diagnosed with tuberculosis or HIV. Laura has written a young adult novel inspired by her experiences in Haiti, called *Hold Tight, Don't Let Go*.

Evans Monsignac lay buried for 27 days — the longest anyone is known to have survived such an ordeal. After being rescued, his weight was recorded at only 88 pounds. He had lost about 60 pounds. When he reflected on his ordeal and his miraculous survival, he said, "Those who are sick should have the courage to live and pray to God, and those who are healthy need to cherish their life and to pray. Now I know that I must live life to the best I can each day."

Evans Monsignac

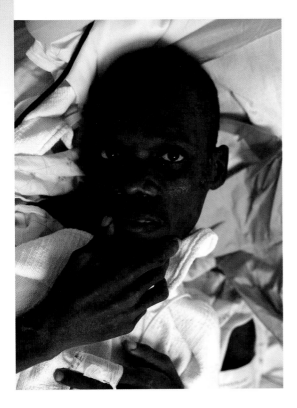

TIMELINE

1492: Columbus first lands on the small island of Hispaniola in the Caribbean Sea and finds it inhabited by Taino Indians.

1697: France takes control of the western one-third of the island, which today is known as Haiti.

1804: Haiti becomes the second nation in the Americas, after the United States, to secure its freedom from colonial rule and, with a population composed almost exclusively of slaves, becomes the first modern black republic.

JANUARY 12, 2010, 4:53 P.M.: A magnitude 7 earthquake shakes the capital city of Port-au-Prince, Haiti, destroying thousands of buildings and homes and killing and injuring hundreds of thousands of people.

JANUARY 12, 2010: In the two hours following the initial earthquake, eight aftershocks with magnitudes between 4.3 and 5.9 rip through the already devastated city of Port-au-Prince.

JANUARY 14, 2010: Lexmark Aristide recovers in Fond Parisien, Haiti, from lifesaving surgery to repair the damage caused by being pinned under the debris of his home.

JANUARY 14, 2010: Former U.S. President Bill Clinton meets with 50 philanthropists in his Harlem, New York, office to discuss how they can help restore Haiti.

JANUARY 15, 2010: Dan Woolley is pulled from the rubble of the Hotel Montana in Port-au-Prince.

JANUARY 15, 2010: Allison Insley-Madsen and her son, Jack, fly back to the United States.

JANUARY 16, 2010: President Obama and former Presidents Bill Clinton and George W. Bush hold a press conference in the Rose Garden outside the White House to announce their plans to help Haiti recover.

JANUARY 18, 2010: Former President Bill Clinton arrives in Port-au-Prince to help deliver humanitarian aid and address the Haitian people.

JANUARY 23, 2010: Wismond Exantus is rescued 11 days after being buried alive under the rubble of the Napoli Hotel.

FEBRUARY 8, 2010: Evans Monsignac is rescued 27 days after being buried alive under the rubble of the La Saline food market, making him the longest-known survivor of an earthquake.

JANUARY 2013: Three years after the Haiti earthquake, nearly 150,000 people continue to live in 271 remaining camps.

2016: Six years after the earthquake, tens of thousands of people still remain homeless in Port-au-Prince.

GLOSSARY

dictatorship (dik-TAY-tuhr-ship)—government by a ruler who took complete control of a country, often unjustly

epicenter (EP-uh-sent-ur)—the point on earth's surface directly above the place where an earthquake occurs

humanitarian (hyoo-MAN-uh-TAIR-ee-uhn)—to care about the needs of other people and provide assistance to those in need

oppression (o-PRESH-uhn)—the treatment of people in a cruel, unjust, and hard way

post-traumatic stress (POHST-traw-MA-tik STRESS)— a condition caused by witnessing or living through a terrifying event that leaves an individual fearful the event might reoccur, resulting in feelings of extreme anxiety and helplessness

revolution (rev-uh-LOO-shun)—an uprising by a group of people against a system of government or a way of life

Richter scale (RIK-tuhr SKALE)—a scale that measures the amount of energy in an earthquake; earthquakes with low numbers cause little or no damage

shock (SHOK)—a medical condition caused by a dangerous drop in blood pressure and flow; people suffering from shock can die

CRITICAL THINKING USING THE COMMON CORE

1. President Préval gave the United States temporary control of the Port-au-Prince airport to allow the coordination of relief efforts immediately following the earthquake. Do you think his decision to do so made the situation better or worse for the victims of the earthquake? Use evidence from the text to support your answer. (Key Ideas and Details)

2. Consider the hardships experienced by the survivors of the 2010 earthquake in Haiti. How are these hardships similar to those experienced by survivors of Hurricane Katrina in the United States? How are they different? (Integration of Knowledge and Ideas)

3. Some of the rescuers refused to save Dan Woolley despite knowing he was trapped alive in the rubble beneath them. Why do you think they would choose not to try to rescue him? Do you think their decision to not attempt a rescue of Dan was justified? Use examples from the text to support your answer. (Key Ideas and Details)

INTERNET SITES

FactHound offers a safe, fun way to find Internet sites related to this book. All of the sites on FactHound have been researched by our staff.

Here's all you do:
Visit *www.facthound.com*
Type in this code: 9781515736066

FactHound will fetch the best sites for you!

FURTHER READING

Benoit, Peter. *The Haitian Earthquake of 2010*. New York: Children's Press, 2012.

Collins, Terry. *Buried in Rubble: True Stories of Surviving Earthquakes*. North Mankato, Minn.: Capstone Press, 2016.

Raum, Elizabeth. *Haiti*. Countries Around the World. Chicago: Heinemann Library, 2012.

Wagner, Laura Rose. *Hold Tight, Don't Let Go: A Novel of Haiti*. New York: Amulet Books, 2015.

SELECTED BIBLIOGRAPHY

Bakody, Jennifer. "A Haitian Father's Account of the Earthquake and Its Aftermath." UNICEF. February 19, 2010. http://www2.unicef.org:60090/infobycountry/haiti_52806.html

Cooper, Helene. "A Presidential Triple Plea for Haiti Relief Fund." *The New York Times*. January 16, 2010. http://thecaucus.blogs.nytimes.com/2010/01/16/a-presidential-triple-plea-for-haiti-relief-fund

Girard, Philippe. *Haiti: The Tumultuous History — From Pearl of the Caribbean to Broken Nation*. New York: Palgrave Macmillan, 2010.

"Haiti: Five Years After Devastating Earthquake Tens of Thousands Still Homeless and Desperate." Amnesty International. January 8, 2015. https://www.amnesty.org/en/latest/news/2015/01/haiti-five-years-after-devastating-earthquake-tens-thousands-still-homeless-and-desperate

Katz, Jonathan M. *The Big Truck That Went By: How the World Came to Save Haiti and Left Behind a Disaster*. New York: Palgrave Macmillan, 2013.

Rucker, Philip. "Haiti Holds a Special Place in the Hearts of Bill and Hillary Clinton." *The Washington Post*. January 16, 2010. http://www.washingtonpost.com/wp-dyn/content/article/2010/01/15/AR2010011503820.html

Wagner, Laura. "Haiti: A Survivor's Story." *Salon*. February 1, 2010. http://www.salon.com/2010/02/02/haiti_trapped_under_the_rubble

Woolley, Dan, and Jennifer Schuchmann. *Unshaken: Rising from the Ruins of Haiti's Hotel Montana*. Grand Rapids, Mich.: Zondervan, 2010.

INDEX

ABOUT THE AUTHOR

Jessica Freeburg lives in Lakeville, Minnesota, with her husband and three children. Her poetry and short stories have appeared in various magazines and anthologies. Her books include fiction and nonfiction for adults, young adults, and middle grade readers. She enjoys allowing her fascination with history to inspire her creatively, working on documentary film production, and traveling to historic locations to experience the past firsthand. You can visit her online at www. jessicafreeburg.com or follow her on Twitter: @jessicafreeburg.